March of America Facsimile Series

Number 42

The Journal of
Major George Washington

George Washington

The Journal of
Major George Washington
by George Washington

ANN ARBOR

UNIVERSITY MICROFILMS, INC.

A Subsidiary of Xerox Corporation

E
312.23
$W27$
1966

Foreword

Between October 31, 1753, and January 16, 1754, George Washington made an extraordinary journey to deliver an ultimatum from Governor Robert Dinwiddie of Virginia to the commandant of the French forces on the Ohio. Washington found the French officer, Captain Jacques Legardeur de St. Pierre at Fort Le Boeuf (now Waterford, Pennsylvania), delivered his letter, received a courteous refusal from the French to get out of the Ohio Valley, returned after terrible hardships to Williamsburg, and delivered his report to Governor Dinwiddie, who ordered it immediately printed. *The Journal of Major George Washington* (Williamsburg, 1754) at once stirred excitement in Virginia, and a copy, sent to London, was reprinted in the same year by Thomas Jefferys. The document served as propaganda to arouse both the colonists and the English to the danger of the French invasion of the Ohio Valley. That was Governor Dinwiddie's purpose in rushing the *Journal* into print.

Virginians in the mid-eighteenth century were eagerly looking to the west for fresh land, and speculative fever was already running high. The Ohio Company and other land companies were organized to settle land in the Ohio Valley which Virginia claimed by reason of her charter granting rights to territory from ocean to ocean. But the French also claimed the same region by right of discovery, and in 1749 the Governor of Canada had sent Captain Céleron de Blainville (or Bienville) to conduct an expedition through the Ohio country to stake French claims by burying lead plates at strategic points inscribed with the French notice of possession. The French also began to move south from Lake Erie and to establish forts. To counter this move, the Virginians also planned bases in the Ohio Valley. On his journey to the French commandant, young George Washington made observations of the best sites for fortifications and reported that the junction of the Allegheny and the Monongahela rivers (the present site of Pittsburgh) offered a particularly favorable site. Unhappily, before the Virginians could complete a fort there, the French arrived in force and drove them off. This came after the events described in Washington's *Journal*, which recounts the hardships he and Christopher Gist, explorer and scout, endured in their winter journey to deliver Dinwiddie's message to the French commandant.

In the preface to the *Journal*, Washington explained that only one day intervened "between my Arrival in Williamsburg and the Time for the Council's Meeting, for me to prepare and transcribe from the rough Minutes I had taken in my Travels this Journal." He apologizes for the rough state of the draft, which he had written merely for the Governor's eye without dreaming that it would be published. He states, however, that "Those Things which came under the Notice of my own Observation, I have been explicit and just in a recital of: Those which I have gathered from Report, I have been particularly cautious not to augment, but ...selected from the whole the most probable and consistent Account."

The *Journal* has been often reprinted. Randolph G. Adams provides a scholarly and succinct introduction to the Scholar's Facsimiles and Reprints edition (New York, 1940). The best discussion of the background of the *Journal* will be found in Douglas Southall Freeman, *George Washington: A Biography*, I (New York, 1948), pp. 274-326.

The Journal of
Major George Washington

THE
JOURNAL
OF
MAJOR *George Washington,*

SENT BY THE

Hon. ROBERT DINWIDDIE, Efq;
His Majefty's Lieutenant-Governor, and
Commander in Chief of *Virginia;*

TO THE

COMMANDANT of the *French* Forces

ON

O H I O.

To which are added, the

GOVERNOR'S LETTER:

AND A

TRANSLATION of the *French* Officer's Anfwer;

WITH

A New MAP of the Country as far as the
M I S S I S S I P P I.

WILLIAMSBURGH Printed,
LONDON, Reprinted for *T. Jefferys,* the Corner
of St. *Martin's Lane.*

MDCCLIV.
[Price One Shilling.]

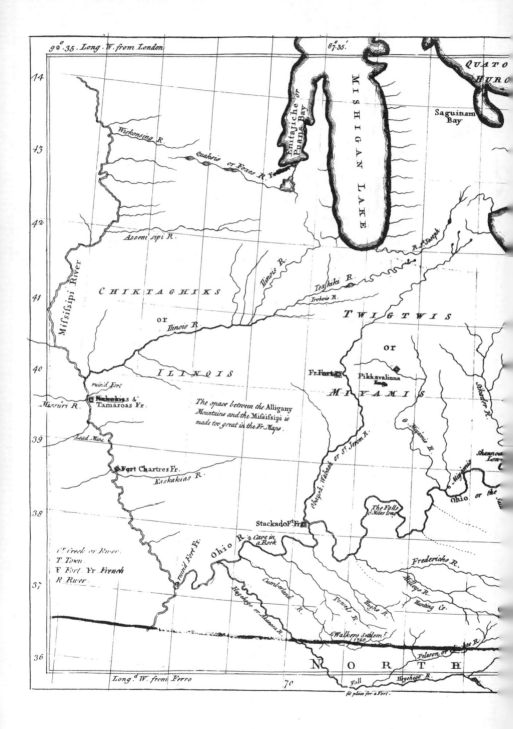

87.35'

QUATO
HURO

14

MISHIGAN LAKE

Saguinam
Bay

43

Weskonsing R.

Ouahsie or Foxes R.

Enitajiche or
Puans Bay

42

Assenisipi R.

R.St Joseph

Mifsifsipi River

CHIKTAGHIKS

Ilinois R.

Teakiki R.

Irohois R.

41

or
Ilinois R.

TWIGTWIS

40

ruin'd Fort

ILINOIS

Fr. Fort

Pikkavalinna

or

MIYAMIS

Missuri R.

Nikhakias &
Tamaroas Fr.

The space between the Alligany
Mountains and the Mifsifsipi is
made too great in the Fr. Maps.

Ohaipi, Wabash or St. Jerom R.

Migiami R.

39

Lead Mine

Shannoa
Low

Fort Chartres Fr.

Kaskakias R.

Ohio or the Sau

38

The Falls
10. Miles long.

Ohio R.

Stackado F. Fr.

37

Cc Creek or River.
T Town.
F Fort. Fr. French.
R River.

ruind Fort. Fr.

Ohio R.

Cave in
a Rock

Frederiks R.

Millago R.

Hunting Cr.

Cumberland R.

Pomink R.

Hogho R.

36

Hogehege or Shawanos R.

Walkers Settlem't
1750

Pelison or ... ees R.

NORTH

70

Fall

Hogehege R.

fit place for a Fort.

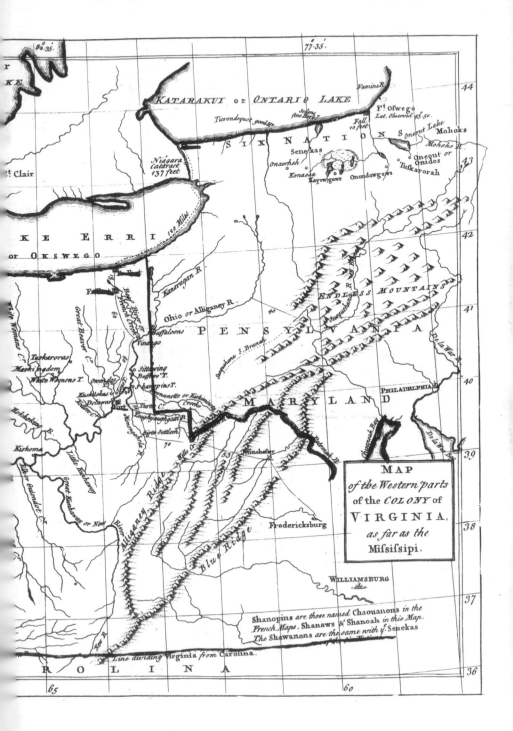

84°.35'.

77°35'.

44

KATARAKUI or ONTARIO LAKE   Famine R.

Ticronodequot good W.   Salens
fine Hort.   Fr Oswego
Lat. Observed 43°.50.

Fall
10 feet   Sonejut Lake   Mohoks

S I X   N A T I O N   Mohoks R.

Senekas   Mohoks R.

St Clair   Niagara
Cataract
137 feet   Onawheh   Onejut or
Onidos

Konassia   Tuskarorah

Kayowigaws   Onondawgaws

42

KE   E R R I   120 Miles

or OKSWEGO   Kanavagan R.

E N D L E S S   M O U N T A I N S   VIRGINIA

41

White Womans Cr.   Bejf Riv.r or
French Creek   60   Ohio or Alliganey R.   40   Susquehanna R. or Majr

Turkororas   Great Beaver Cr.   Buffaloons   P E N S Y L V A N I A

Maski ingdom   60   Vinango   Susphona S. Branch   De la War

White Womens T.   Onondas   Sittening
Buffalo T.   40

Kaskaskas   Shamppins T.   MARYLAND   PHILADELPHIA

Delaware   Kishiminetto or Kishiming

Hokhokiney R.   Turtle Cr.   Creek.   De la War Bay

Kiskoma   Loughughgan   39

Firts Settlem.   Winchefter   Potomak R.   Chisapeak Bay

Kiskoma   70   Mille Cr.   53   MAP

or New   Fredericksburg   of the Western parts
of the COLONY of
VIRGINIA,
as far as the
Mifsifsipi.

38

Blue Ridge   Fredericksburg

WILLIAMSBURG   37

Shanopins are those named Chaouanons in the
French Maps, Shanaws & Shanoah in this Map.
The Shawanons are the same with ye Senekas

ROLINA   Line dividing Virginia from Carolina.   36

65   60

Maps, Plans *and* Charts *juſt imported by* Thomas Jefferys, *Geographer to his Royal Highneſs the* Prince *of* Wales.

LE Indies Orientale, avec le cote de Coromandel, et l'Analiſe par M. D. Anville.

Novelles Cartes de les Indies Orientale par M. D'apres de de Mannivellette.

Theatre de la Guerre in Italic par M. D'Anville, prem: Partie.

Mappemende de M. Boulanſger avec ſon Memóire, in Quarto.

Memoire ſur les nov. decouveiter de l'Amiral de Fonte, avec Cartes

Confiderations Geographiques : in Quarto, avec 4 Cartes par M. Buache.

Canada de Robert, 1753.

Porter de France par Jalliot, 1754.

Dekiles Atlas complete, large Paper and ſmall.

The German Atlas compleat by Homan.

Atlas de France, 1751.

The Chineſe Atlas by D'Anville.

The Ruſſian Atlas compiled and engraved at Peterſburgh.

D'Anvilles's new Maps of Italy, North America, South America, Africa and the Eaſtward Part of Aſia

Bellin's Sea Charts.

Plan of Rome
——— Venice
——— Berlin
——— Environs of Paris, 9 Sheets
——— Paris, one Sheet
——— the Military School
——— Verſailles, one Sheet
——— Marly
——— Nancy
——— l'Orient

Speedily will be publiſhed.

A Map of the Seat of War in the *Eaſt Indies*, with a Memoir.

ADVERTISEMENT.

AS it was thought adviseable by his Honour the Governor to have the following Account of my Proceedings to and from the French on Ohio, committed to Print; I think I can do no less than apologize, in some Measure, for the numberless Imperfections of it.

There intervened but one Day between my Arrival in Williamsburg, and the Time for the Council's Meeting, for me to prepare and transcribe, from the rough Minutes I had taken in my Travels, this Journal; the writing of which only was sufficient to employ me closely the whole Time, consequently admitted of no Leisure to consult of a new and proper Form to offer it in, or to correct or amend the Diction of the old : Neither was I apprised, nor did in the least conceive,

when

ADVERTISEMENT.

when I wrote this for his Honour's Perusal, that it ever would be published, or even have more than a cursory Reading; till I was informed, at the Meeting of the present General Assembly, that it was already in the Press.

There is nothing can recommend it to the Public, but this. Those Things which came under the Notice of my own Observation, I have been explicit and just in a Recital of:——Those which I have gathered from Report, I have been particularly cautious not to augment, but collected the Opinions of the several Intelligencers, and selected from the whole, the most probable and consistent Account.

G. WASHINGTON.

THE

JOURNAL, &c.

Wednesday, October 31st, 1753.

I WAS commiſſioned and appointed by the Honourable *Robert Dinwiddie*, Eſq; Governor, &c. of *Virginia*, to viſit and deliver a Letter to the Commandant of the *French* Forces on the *Ohio*, and ſet out on the intended Journey the ſame Day : The next, I arrived at *Frederickſburg*, and engaged Mr. *Jacob Van-braam*, to be my *French* Interpreter ; and proceeded with him to *Alexandria*, where we provided Neceſſaries. From thence we went to *Wincheſter*, and got Baggage, Horſes, &c. and from thence we purſued the new Road to *Wills-Creek*, where we arrived the 14th of *November*.

Here I engaged Mr. *Giſt* to pilot us out, and alſo hired four others as Servitors, *Barnaby Currin*, and

and *John Mac-Quire*, Indian Traders, *Henry Steward*, and *William Jenkins* ; and in Company with those Persons, left the Inhabitants the Day following.

The excessive Rains and vast Quantity of Snow which had fallen, prevented our reaching Mr. *Frazier*'s, an Indian Trader, at the Mouth of *Turtle*-Creek, on *Monongahela* [River] till *Thursday* the 22d. We were informed here, that Expresses had been sent a few Days before to the Traders down the River, to acquaint them with the *French* General's Death, and the Return of the major Part of the *French* Army into Winter Quarters.

The Waters were quite impassable, without swimming our Horses ; which obliged us to get the Loan of a Canoe from *Frazier*, and to send *Barnaby Currin*, and *Henry Steward*, down the *Monongahela*, with our Baggage, to meet us at the Forks of *Ohio*, about 10 Miles, there to cross the *Aligany*.*

As I got down before the Canoe, I spent some Time in viewing the Rivers, and the Land in the Fork ; which I think extremely well situated for a Fort, as it has the absolute Command of both Rivers. The Land at the Point is 20 or 25 Feet above the common Surface of the Water ; and a considerable Bottom of flat, well-timbered Land all around it, very convenient for Building : The Rivers are each a Quarter of a Mile, or more, across, and run here very near at right Angles : *Aligany* bearing N. E. and *Monongahela* S. E. The former of these two is a very rapid and swift running Water ; the other deep and still, without any perceptible Fall.

About two Miles from this, on the South East Side of the River, at the Place where the *Ohio*

* The *Ohio* and *Aligany* are the same River.

Company

Company intended to erect a Fort, lives *Shingifs*, King of the *Delawares* : We called upon him, to invite him to Council at the *Loggs*-Town.

As I had taken a good deal of Notice Yefterday of the Situation at the *Forks*, my Curiofity led me to examine this more particularly, and I think it greatly inferior, either for Defence or Advantages ; efpecially the latter : For a Fort at the *Forks* would be equally well fituated on the *Ohio*, and have the entire Command of the *Monongahela* ; which runs up to our Settlements and is extremely well defigned for Water Carriage, as it is of a deep ftill Nature. Befides a Fort at the *Fork* might be built at a much lefs Expence, than at the other Place.—

Nature has well contrived this lower Place, for Water Defence ; but the Hill whereon it muft ftand being about a Quarter of a Mile in Length, and then defcending gradually on the Land Side, will render it difficult and very expenfive, to make a fufficient Fortification there.—The whole Flat upon the Hill muft be taken-in, the Side next the Defcent made extremely high, or elfe the Hill itfelf cut away : Otherwife, the Enemy may raife Batteries within that Diftance without being expofed to a fingle Shot from the Fort.

Shingifs attended us to the *Loggs*-Town, where we arrived between Sun-fetting and Dark, the 25th Day after I left *Williamfburg*. We travelled over fome extreme good and bad Land, to get to this Place.—

As foon as I came into Town, I went to *Monakatoocha* (as the Half-king was out at his hunting-Cabbin on little *Beaver*-Creek, about 15 Miles off) and informed him by *John Davifon* my *Indian* Interpreter, that I was fent a Meffenger to the *French* General ; and was ordered to call upon the Sachems of the *Six Nations*, to acquaint them with
it.—

it.—I gave him a String of Wampum †, and a
Twift of Tobacco, and defired him to fend for the
Half-King ; which he promifed to do by a Runner
in the Morning, and for other Sachems.—I invited
him and the other great Men prefent to my Tent,
where they ftay'd about an Hour and return'd.

According to the beft Obfervations I could make,
Mr. *Giff*'s new Settlement (which we pafs'd by)
bears about W. N. W. 70 Miles from *Wills*-Creek ;
Shanapins, or the Forks N. by W. or N. N. W.
about 50 Miles from that ; and from thence to the
Loggs-Town, the Courfe is nearly Weft about 18
or 20 Miles: So that the whole Diftance, as we
went and computed it, is at leaft 135 or 140 Miles
from our back Inhabitants.

25*th*, Came to Town four of ten *Frenchmen* who
had deferted from a Company at the *Kufkufkas*, which
lies at the Mouth of this River. I got the following Account from them. They were fent from
New-Orleans with 100 Men, and 8 Canoe-Loads
of Provifions to this Place ; where they expected to
have met the fame Number of Men, from the Forts
on this Side Lake *Erie*, to convoy them and the
Stores up, who were not arrived when they ran-off.

I enquired into the Situation of the *French*, on
the *Miffiffippi*, their Number, and what Forts they
had built. They inform'd me, That there were
four fmall Forts between *New-Orleans* and the
Black-Iflands, garrifon'd with about 30 or 40 Men,
and a few fmall Pieces in each: That at *New-Orleans*, which is near the Mouth of the *Miffiffippi*,
there are 35 Companies, of 40 Men each, with a
pretty ftrong Fort mounting 8 Carriage Guns ; and
at the *Black-Iflands* there are feveral Companies,
and a Fort with 6 Guns. The *Black-Iflands* are

† A kind of *Indian* Money ; alfo given as a Prefent or Mark
of Friendfhip.

about

about 130 Leagues above the Mouth of the *Ohio,*
which is about 350 above *New-Orleans.* They alſo
acquainted me, that there was a ſmall pallifado'd
Fort on the *Ohio,* at the Mouth of the *Obaiſh* about
60 Leagues from the *Miſſiſipi.* The *Obaiſh* * heads
near the Weſt End of Lake *Erie,* and affords the
Communication between the *French* on *Miſſiſſippi*
and thoſe on the Lakes. Theſe Deſerters came up
from the lower *Shanoah* Town with one *Brown,* an
Indian Trader, and were going to *Philadelphia.*

About 3 o'Clock this Evening the Half-King
came to Town. I went up and invited him with
Daviſon, privately, to my Tent ; and deſir'd him
to relate ſome of the Particulars of his Journey to
the *French* Commandant, and Reception there :
Alſo to give me an Account of the Ways and Diftance. He told me, that the neareſt and levelleſt
Way was now impaſſable, by Reaſon of many large
mirey Savannas ; that we muſt be obliged to go by
Venango, and ſhould not get to the near Fort under
5 or 6 Nights Sleep, good Travelling. When he
went to the Fort, he ſaid he was received in a very
ſtern Manner by the late Commander ; Who aſk'd
him very abruptly, what he had come about, and
to declare his Buſineſs : Which he ſaid he did in the
following Speech.

Fathers, I am come to tell you your own Speeches ;
what your own Mouths have declared. Fathers, You,
in former Days, ſet a Silver Baſon before us, wherein
there was the Leg of a Beaver, and deſir'd all the
Nations to come and eat of it ; to eat in Peace and
Plenty, and not to be churliſh to one another : And
that if any ſuch Perſon ſhould be found to be a Dif-
turber, I here lay down by the Edge of the Diſh a

* Or *Wabaſh,* written by the *French Ouabach.*

B   *Rod,*

Rod, which you muſt ſcourge them with ; and if I your Father, ſhould get fooliſh, in my old Days, {I deſire you may uſe it upon me as well as others.

Now Fathers, it is you who are the Diſturbers in this Land, by coming and building your Towns; and taking it away unknown to us, and by Force.

Fathers, We kindled a Fire a long Time ago, at a Place called Montreal, *where we deſired you to ſtay, and not to come and intrude upon our Land. I now deſire you may diſpatch to that Place ; for be it known to you, Fathers, that this is our Land, and not yours.*

Fathers, I deſire you may hear me in Civilneſs ; if not, we muſt handle that Rod which was laid down for the Uſe of the abſtreperous. If you had come in a peaceable Manner, like our Brothers the Engliſh, *we ſhould not have been againſt your trading with us, as they do ;* BUT TO COME, FATHERS, AND BUILD HOUSES UPON OUR LAND, AND TO TAKE IT BY FORCE, IS WHAT WE CANNOT SUBMIT TO.

Fathers, Both you and the Engliſh *are white, we live in a Country between ; therefore the Land belongs to neither one nor t'other : But the Great Being above allow'd it to be a Place of Reſidence for us ; ſo Fathers, I deſire you to withdraw, as I have done our Brothers the* Engliſh : *For I will keep you at Arms length. I lay this down as a Trial for both, to ſee which will have the greateſt Regard to it, and that Side we will ſtand by, and make equal Sharers with us. Our Brothers the* Engliſh *have heard this, and I come now to tell it to you ; for I am not afraid to diſcharge you off this Land.*

This he ſaid was the Subſtance of what he ſpoke to the General, who made this Reply.

Now

Now my Child, I have heard your Speech: You spoke first, but it is my Time to speak now. Where is my Wampum that you took away, with the Marks of Towns in it? This Wampum I do not know, which you have discharged me off the Land with: But you need not put yourself to the Trouble of speaking, for I will not hear you. I am not afraid of Flies, or Musquitos, for Indians *are such as those. I tell you, down that River I will go, and will build upon it, according to my Command. If the River was block'd up, I have Forces sufficient to burst it open, and tread under my Feet all that stand in Opposition, together with their Alliances; for my Force is as the Sand upon the Sea Shore: Therefore, here is your Wampum, I fling it at you. Child, you talk foolish; you say this Land belongs to you, but there is not the Black of my Nail yours. I saw that Land sooner than you did, before the Shannoahs and you were at* War: Lead *was the Man who went down, and took Possession of that River: It is my Land, and I will have it, let who will stand-up for, or say-against, it. I'll buy and sell with the* English, *(mockingly). If People will be rul'd by me, they may expect Kindness, but not else.*

The Half-King told me he enquired of the General after two *Englishmen* who were made Prisoners, and received this Answer.

Child, You think it is a very great Hardship that I made Prisoners of those two People at Venango. *Don't you concern yourself with it: We took and carried them to* Canada, *to get Intelligence of what the* English *were doing in* Virginia.

He informed me that they had built two Forts, one on Lake *Erie,* and another on *French*-Creek,

near

near a small Lake about 15 Miles asunder, and a large Waggon Road between : They are both built after the same Model, but different in the Size ; that on the Lake the largest. He gave me a Plan of them, of his own drawing.

The *Indians* enquired very particularly after their Brothers in *Carolina* Goal.

They also asked what Sort of a Boy it was who was taken from the *South*-Branch ; for they were told by some *Indians*, that a Party of *French Indians* had carried a white Boy by the *Kuskuska* Town, towards the Lakes.

26*th*. We met in Council at the *Long-House*, about 9 o'Clock, where I spoke to them as follows.

Brothers, I have called you together in Council, by Order of your Brother the Governor of Virginia, to acquaint you, that I am sent, with all possible Dispatch, to visit, and deliver a Letter to the French Commandant, of very great Importance to your Brothers the English ; *and I dare say, to you their Friends and Allies.*

I was desired, Brothers, by your Brother the Governor, to call upon you, the Sachems of the Nations, to inform you of it, and to ask your Advice and Assistance to proceed the nearest and best Road to the French. *You see, Brothers, I have gotten thus far on my Journey.*

His Honour likewise desired me to apply to you for some of your young Men, to conduct and provide Provisions for us on our Way; and be a Safeguard against those French Indians *who have taken up the Hatchet against us. I have spoke this particularly to you, Brothers, because his Honour our Governor treats you as good Friends and Allies; and holds you in great Esteem.*

Eſteem. To confirm what I have ſaid, I give you this String of Wampum.

After they had conſider:d for ſome Time on the above Diſcourſe, the Half-King got up and ſpoke.

Now, my Brothers, in Regard to what my Brother the Governor has deſired me, I return you this Anſwer.

I rely upon you as a Brother ought to do, as you ſay we are Brothers and one People: We ſhall put Heart in Hand, and ſpeak to our Fathers the French concerning the Speech they made to me ; and you may depend that we will endeavour to be your Guard.

Brother, as you have aſked my Advice, I hope you will be ruled by it, and ſtay till I can provide a Company to go with you. The French Speech-Belt is not here, I have it to go for to my hunting-Cabbin: Likewiſe the People whom I have ordered in, are not yet come, nor cannot till the third Night from this ; till which Time, Brother, I muſt beg you to ſtay.

I intend to ſend a Guard of Mingo's, Shannoahs, *and* Delawares, *that our Brothers may ſee the Love and Loyalty we bear them.*

As I had Orders to make all poſſible Diſpatch, and waiting here was very contrary to my Inclination, I thanked him in the moſt ſuitable Manner I could; and told him, that my Buſineſs required the greateſt Expedition, and would not admit of that Delay. He was not well pleaſed that I ſhould offer to go before the Time he had appointed, and told me, that he could not conſent to our going without a Guard, for Fear ſome Accident ſhould befal us, and draw a Reflection upon him. Beſides, ſays he, this is a Matter of no ſmall Moment, and muſt

not

not be entered into without due Confideration : For
now I intend to deliver up the *French*-Speech-Belt,
and make the *Shanoahs* and *Delawares* do the
fame. And accordingly he gave Orders to King
Shingifs, who was prefent, to attend on *Wednefday*
Night with the Wampum; and two Men of their
Nation to be in Readinefs to fet-out with us next
Morning. As I found it was impoffible to get-off
without affronting them in the moft egregious
Manner, I confented to ftay.

I gave them back a String of Wampum which I
met with at Mr. *Frezier*'s, and which they had fent
with a Speech to his Honour the Governor, to
inform him, that three Nations of *French Indians*,
viz. *Chippoways*, *Ottoways*, and *Orundaks*, had
taken-up the Hatchet againft the *Englifh*; and defired them to repeat it over again : But this they
poftponed doing till they met in full Council with
the *Shannoahs* and *Delaware* Chiefs.

27*th*. Runners were difpatched very early for
the *Shannoah* Chiefs. The Half-King fet out himfelf
to fetch the *French*-Speech-Belt from his hunting
Cabbin.

28*th*. He returned this Evening, and came with
Monokatoocha, and two other Sachems to my Tent;
and begged (as they had complied with his Honour the Governor's Requeft, in providing Men,
&c.) to know on what Bufinefs we were going to
the *French ?* this was a Queftion I all along expected, and had provided as fatisfactory Anfwers
to, as I could ; which allayed their Curiofity a
little.

Monokatoocha informed me, that an *Indian* from
Venango brought News, a few Days ago, that the
French had called all the *Mingo*'s, *Delawares*, &c.
together at that Place; and told them, that they
intended

intended to have been down the River this Fall,
but the Waters were growing cold, and the Winter
advancing, which obliged them to go into Quarters :
But that they might affuredly expect them in the
Spring, with a far greater Number ; and defired
that they might be quite paffive, and not to in-
termeddle, unlefs they had a Mind to draw all
their Force upon them : For that they expected to
fight the *Englifh* three Years (as they fuppofed there
would be fome Attempts made to ftop them) in
which Time they fhould conquer : But that if
they fhould prove equally ftrong, they and the
Englifh, would join to cut them all off, and divide
the Land between them : That though they had
loft their General, and fome few of their Soldiers,
yet there were Men enough to reinforce them,
and make them Mafters of the *Ohio*.

This Speech, he faid, was delivered to them by
one Captain *Joncaire* their Interpreter in Chief,
living at *Venango*, and a Man of Note in the Army.

29*th*. The Half-King and *Monokatoocha*, came
very early, and begged me to ftay one Day more:
For notwithftanding they had ufed all the Diligence
in their Power, the *Shanoah* Chiefs had not brought
the Wampum they ordered, but would certainly
be in To-night ; if not, they would delay me no
longer, but would fend it after us as foon as they
arrived. When I found them fo preffing in
their Requeft, and knew that returning of Wampum was the abolifhing of Agreements ; and
giving this up, was fhaking-off all Dependance
upon the *French*, I confented to ftay, as I believed
an Offence offered at this Crifis, might be attended
with greater ill Confequence, than another Day's
Delay. They alfo informed me, that *Shingifs* could
not get-in his Men ; and was prevented from coming

ing himfelf by his Wife's Sicknefs, (I believe, by
Fear of the *French*); but that the Wampum of that
Nation was lodged with *Kuftaloga* one of their
Chiefs at *Venango*.

In the Evening late they came again and acquainted me that the *Shannoahs* were not yet arrived, but that it fhould not retard the Profecution
of our Journey. He delivered in my Hearing, the
Speeches that were to be made to the *French* by
Jeſkakake, one of their old Chiefs, which was
giving-up the Belt the late Commandant had afked
for, and repeating near the fame Speech he himfelf had done before.

He alfo delivered a String of Wampum to this
Chief, which was fent by King *Shingiſs*, to be given
to *Kuftaloga*, with Orders to repair to the *French*,
and deliver-up the Wampum.

He likewife gave a very large String of black
and white Wampum, which was to be fent up
immediately to the Six Nations, if the *French* refufed to quit the Land at this Warning ; which
was the third and laft Time, and was the Right
of this *Jeſkakake* to deliver.

30th. Laft Night the great Men affembled to
their Council-Houfe, to confult further about this
Journey, and who were to go : The Refult of
which was, that only three of their Chiefs, with
one of their beft Hunters, fhould be our Convoy.
The Reafon they gave for not fending more, after
what had been propofed at Council the 26th, was,
that a greater Number might give the *French* Suf-
picions of fome bad Defign, and caufe them to
be treated rudely : But I rather think they could
not get their Hunters in.

We fet out about 9 o'Clock with the Half-King,
Jeſkakake, *White Thunder*, and the Hunter ; and
travelled

travelled on the Road to *Venango*, where we arrived the 4th of *December*, without any Thing remarkable happening but a continued Series of bad Weather.

This is an old *Indian* Town, fituated at the Mouth of *French* Creek on *Ohio* ; and lies near N. about 60 Miles from the *Loggs*-Town, but more than 70 the Way we were obliged to go.

We found the *French* Colours hoifted at a Houfe from which they had driven Mr. *John Frazier*, an *Englifh* Subject. I immediately repaired to it, to know where the Commander refided. There were three Officers, one of whom, Capt. *Joncaire*, informed me, that he had the Command of the *Ohio* : But that there was a General Officer at the near Fort, where he advifed me to apply for an Anfwer. He invited us to fup with them ; and treated us with the greateft Complaifance.

The Wine, as they dofed themfelves pretty plentifully with it, foon banifhed the Reftraint which at firft appeared in their Converfation ; and gave a Licence to their Tongues to reveal their Sentiments more freely.

They told me, That it was their abfolute Defign to take Poffeffion of the *Ohio*, and by G— they would do it : For that altho' they were fenfible the *Englifh* could raife two Men for their one ; yet they knew, their Motions were too flow and dilatory to prevent any Undertaking of theirs. They pretend to have an undoubted Right to the River, from a Difcovery made by one *La Solle* 60 Years ago ; and the Rife of this Expedition is, to prevent our fettling on the River or Waters of it, as they had heard of fome Families moving-out in Order thereto. From the beft Intelligence I could get, there have been 1500 Men on this Side *Ontario*

C   Lake

Lake : But upon the Death of the General all were
recalled to about 6 or 700, who were left to garrifon four Forts, 150 or there abouts in each. The
firft of them is on *French*-Creek, near a fmall
Lake, about 60 Miles from *Venango*, near N.N.W.
the next lies on Lake *Erie*, where the greater Part
of their Stores are kept, about 15 Miles from the
other. From this it is 120 Miles to the carrying
Place, at the Falls of Lake *Erie*, where there is a
fmall Fort; which they lodge their Goods at, in
bringing them from *Montreal*, the Place whence all
their Stores come from. The next Fort lies about
20 Miles from this, on *Ontario*-Lake. Between
this Fort and *Montreal* there are three others, the
firft of which is near oppofite to the *Englifh* Fort
Ofwego. From the Fort on Lake *Erie* to *Montreal*
is about 600 Miles, which they fay requires no
more, if good Weather, than four Weeks Voyage,
if they go in Barks or large Veffels, fo that they may
crofs the Lake : But if they come in Canoes it will
require 5 or 6 Weeks, for they are obliged to keep
under the Shore.

5th. Rain'd exceffively all Day, which prevented
our Travelling. Capt. *Joncaire* fent for the Half-
King, as he had but juft heard that he came with me:
He affected to be much concerned that I did not
make free to bring them in before. I excufed it in
the beft Manner I was capable, and told him, I
did not think their Company agreeable, as I had
heard him fay a good deal in Difpraife of *Indians* in
general. But another Motive prevented me from
bringing them into his Company : I knew he was
Interpreter, and a Perfon of very great Influence
among the *Indians*, and had lately ufed all poffible
Means to draw them over to their Intereft ; therefore I was defirous of giving no Opportunity that
could be avoided. When

When they came in, there was great Pleafure expreffed at feeing them. He wondred how they could be fo near without coming to vifit him ; made feveral trifling Prefents ; and applied Loquor fo faft, that they were foon rendred incapable of the Bufinefs they came about, notwithftanding the Caution which was given.

6th. The Half-King came to my Tent, quite fober, and infifted very much that I fhould ftay and hear what he had to fay to the *French*. I fain would have prevented his fpeaking any Thing, till he came to the Commandant ; but could not prevail. He told me, that at this Place a Council Fire was kindled, where all their Bufinefs with thefe People was to be tranfacted; and that the Management of the *Indian* Affairs was left folely to Monfieur *Joncaire*. As I was defirous of knowing the Iffue of this, I agreed to ftay: But fent our Horfes a little Way up *French* Creek, to raft over and encamp ; which I knew would make it near Night.

About 10 o'Clock they met in Council. The King fpoke much the fame as he had before done to the General ; and offered the *French* Speech-Belt which had before been demanded, with the Marks of four Towns on it, which Monfieur *Joncaire* refufed to receive ; but defired him to carry it to the Fort to the Commander.

7th. Monfieur *La Force*, Commiffary of the *French* Stores, and three other Soldiers came over to accompany us up. We found it extremely difficult to get the *Indians* off To-day, as every Stratagem had been ufed to prevent their going-up with me. I had laft Night left *John Davifon* (the *Indian* Interpreter whom I brought with me from Town, and ftrictly charged him not to be out of their Company, as I could not get them over to

C 2   my my Tent; for they had some Business with *Kustaloga*, chiefly to know the Reason why he did not deliver up the *French* Belt which he had in Keeping: But I was obliged to send Mr. *Gist* over To-day to fetch them; which he did with great Persuasion.

At 11 o'Clock we set out for the Fort, and were prevented from arriving there till the 11th by excessive Rains, Snows, and bad Travelling, through many Mires and Swamps. These we were obliged to pass, to avoid crossing the Creek, which was impossible, either by fording or rafting, the Water was so high and rapid.

We passed over much good Land since we left *Venango*, and through several extensive and very rich Meadows; one of which I believe was near four Miles in Length, and considerably wide in some Places.

12*th*. I prepared early to wait upon the Commander, and was received and conducted to him by the second Officer in Command. I acquainted him with my Business, and offered my Commission and Letter: Both of which he desired me to keep till the Arrival of Monsieur *Riparti*, Captain, at the next Fort, who was sent for and expected every Hour.

This Commander is a Knight of the military Order of St. *Lewis*, and named *Legardeur de St. Piere*. He is an elderly Gentleman, and has much the Air of a Soldier. He was sent over to take the Command, immediately upon the Death of the late General, and arrived here about seven Days before me.

At 2 o'Clock the Gentleman who was sent for arrived, when I offered the Letter, *&c.* again; which they received, and adjourned into a private Apartment for the Captain to translate, who understood

derftood a little *Englifh*. After he had done it, the
Commander defired I would walk-in, and bring
my Interpreter to perufe and correct it; which
I did.

13th. The chief Officers retired, to hold a Council
of War; which gave me an Opportunity of taking
the Dimenfions of the Fort, and making what Obfervations I could.

It is fituated on the South, or Weft Fork of
French Creek, near the Water; and is almoft fur-
rounded by the Creek, and a fmall Branch of it
which forms a Kind of Ifland. Four Houfes
compofe the Sides. The Baftions are made of Piles
driven into the Ground, ftanding more than 12 Feet
above it, and fharp at Top: With Port-Holes cut
for Cannon, and Loop-Holes for the fmall Arms to
fire through. There are eight 6 *lb.* Pieces mounted,
in each Baftion; and one Piece of four Pound before
the Gate. In the Baftions are a Guard-Houfe,
Chapel, Doctor's Lodging, and the Commander's
private Store: Round which are laid Plat-Forms for
the Cannon and Men to ftand on. There are feveral
Barracks without the Fort, for the Soldiers Dwell-
ing; covered, fome with Bark, and fome with
Boards, made chiefly of Loggs. There are alfo
feveral other Houfes, fuch as Stables, Smiths
Shop, *&c.*

I could get no certain Account of the Number
of Men here : But according to the beft Judgment
I could form, there are an Hundred exclufive of
Officers, of which there are many. I alfo gave
Orders to the People who were with me, to take
an exact Account of the Canoes which were hauled-
up to convey their Forces down in the Spring.
This they did, and told 50 of Birch Bark, and
170 of Pine; befides many others which were block-
ed-out, in Readinefs to make. *14th.* As

14*th.* As the Snow encreafed very faft, and our Horfes daily became weaker, I fent them off unloaded; under the Care of *Barnaby Currin* and two others, to make all convenient Difpatch to *Venango*, and there wait our Arrival, if there was a Pofpect of the Rivers freezing: If not, then to continue down to *Shanapin's* Town, at the Forks of *Ohio*, and there to wait till we came to crofs *Aliganey*; intending myfelf to go down by Water, as I had the Offer of a Canoe or two.

As I found many Plots concerted to retard the *Indians* Bufinefs, and prevent their returning with me; I endeavour'd all that lay in my Power to fruftrate their Schemes, and hurry them on to execute their intended Defign. They accordingly preffed for Admittance this Evening, which at Length was granted them, privately, with the Commander and one or two other Officers. The Half-King told me, that he offer'd the Wampum to the Commander, who evaded taking it, and made many fair Promifes of Love and Friendfhip; faid he wanted to live in Peace, and trade amicably with them, as a Proof of which he would fend fome Goods immediately down to the *Logg's-*Town for them. But I rather think the Defign of that is, to bring away all our ftraggling Traders they meet with, as I privately underftood they intended to carry an Officer, &*c.* with them. And what rather confirms this Opinion, I was enquiring of the Commander, by what Authority he had made Prifoners of feveral of our *Englifh* Subjects. He told me that the Country belong'd to them; that no *Englifhman* had a Right to trade upon thofe Waters; and that he had Orders to make every Perfon Prifoner who attempted it on the *Ohio*, or the Waters of it.

I

I enquir'd of Capt. *Riparti* about the Boy who was carried by this Place, as it was done while the Command devolved on him, between theDeath of the late General, and the Arrival of the prefent. He acknowledged, that a Boy had been carried paft; and that the *Indians* had two or three white Men's Scalps, (I wastold by fome of the *Indians* at *Venango* Eight) but pretended to have forgotten the Name of the Place which the Boy came from, and all the Particular Facts, though he had queftion'd him for fome Hours, as they were carrying him paft. I likewife enquired what they had done with *John Trotter* and *James Mac Clocklan*, two *Penfylvania* Traders, whom they had taken, with all their Goods. They told me, that they had been fent to *Canada*, but were now returned Home.

This Evening I received an Anfwer to his Honour the Governor's Letter from the Commandant.

15*th,* The Commandant ordered a plentiful Store of Liquor, Provifion, *&c.* to be put on Board our Canoe ; and appeared to be extremely complaifant, though he wasexerting every Artifice which he could invent to fet our own *Indians* at Variance with us, to prevent their going 'till after our Departure. Prefents, Rewards, and every Thing which could be fuggefted by him or his Officers.——I can't fay that ever in my Life I fuffer'd fo much Anxiety as I did in this Affair : I faw that every Stratagem which the moft fruitful Brain could invent, was practifed, to win the Half-King to their Intereft; and that leaving him here was giving them the Opportunity they aimed at,——I went to the Half-King and prefs'd him in the ftrongeft Terms to go: He told me the Commandant would not difcharge him 'till the Morning. I then went to the Commandant, and defired him to do their Bufinefs; and complain'd

of

of ill Treatment: For keeping them, as they were Part of my Company, was detaining me. This he promised not to do, but to forward my Journey as much as he could. He protested he did not keep them, but was ignorant of the Cause of their Stay; though I soon found it out:——He had promised them a present of Guns, &c. if they would wait 'till the Morning.

As I was very much prefs'd, by the *Indians*, to wait this Day for them, I confented, on a Promife, That nothing fhould hinder them in the Morning.

16*th*. The *French* were not flack in their Inventions to keep the *Indians* this Day alfo: But as they were obligated, according to Promife, to give the Prefent, they then endeavoured to try the Power of Liquor; which I doubt not would have prevailed at any other Time than this: But I urged and infifted with the King fo clofely upon his Word, that he refrained, and fet-off with us as he had engaged.

We had a tedious and very fatiguing Paffage down the Creek. Several Times we had like to have been ftaved againft Rocks; and many Times were obliged all Hands to get-out and remain in the Water Half an Hour or more, getting over the Shoals. At one Place the Ice had lodged and made it impaffable by Water; therefore we were obliged to carry our Canoe acrofs a Neck of Land, a Quarter of a Mile over. We did not reach *Venango*, till the 22d, where we met with our Horfes.

This Creek is extremely crooked, I dare fay the Diftance between the Fort and *Venango* can't be lefs than 130 Miles, to follow the Meanders.

23*d*, When I got Things ready to fet-off, I fent for the Half-King, to know whether he intended to go with us, or by Water. He told me that *White-Thunder* had hurt himfelf much, and was fick and unable

unable to walk; therefore he was obliged to carry him down in a Canoe. As I found he intended to ſtay here a Day or two, and knew that Monſieur *Joncaire* would employ every Scheme to ſet him againſt the *Engliſh* as he had before done; I told him I hoped he would guard againſt his Flattery, and let no fine Speeches influence him in their Favour. He deſired I might not be concerned, for he knew the *French* too well, for any Thing to engage him in their Behalf; and that though he could not go down with us, he yet would endeavour to meet at the Forks with *Joſeph Campbell*, to deliver a Speech for me to carry to his Honour the Governor. He told me he would order the young Hunter to attend us, and get Proviſion, &c. if wanted.

Our Horſes were now ſo weak and feeble, and the Baggage ſo heavy (as we were obliged to provide all the Neceſſaries which the Journey would require) that we doubted much their performing it: therefore myſelf and others (except the Drivers who were obliged to ride) gave-up our Horſes for Packs, to aſſiſt along with the Baggage. I put myſelf in an *Indian* walking Dreſs, and continued with them three Days, till I found there was no Probability of their getting home in any reaſonable Time. The Horſes grew leſs able to travel every Day; the Cold increaſed very faſt; and the Roads were becoming much worſe by a deep Snow, continually freezing: Therefore as I was uneaſy to get back, to make Report of my Proceedings to his Honour the Governor, I determined to proſecute my Journey the neareſt Way through the Woods, on Foot.

Accordingly I left Mr. *Vanbraam* in Charge of our Baggage; with Money and Directions, to provide Neceſſaries from Place to Place for themſelves

D and

and Horfes, and to make the moft convenient Di-
patch in Travelling.

I took my neceffary Papers ; pulled-off my
Cloaths ; and tied myfelf up in a Match Coat. Then
with Gun in Hand and Pack at my Back, in which
were my Papers and Provifions, I fet-out with Mr.
Gift, fitted in the fame Manner, on *Wednefday* the
26th. The Day following, juft after we had paffed
a Place called the *Murdering*-Town (where we intended to quit the Path, and fteer acrofs the Country
for *Shannapins* Town)we fell-in with a Party of *French*
Indians, who had lain in Wait for us. One of them
fired at Mr. *Gift* or me, not 15 Steps off, but fortunately miffed. We took this Fellow into Cuftody,
and kept him till about 9 o'Clock at Night :
Then let him go, and walked all the remaining Part
of the Night without making any Stop ; that we
might get the Start, fo far, as to be out of the
Reach of their Purfuit the next Day, fince we were
well affured they would follow our Tract as foon as
it was light. The next Day we continued travelling
till quite dark, and got to the River about two Miles
above *Shannapins*. We expected to have found the
River frozen, but it was not, only about 50 Yards
from each Shore : The Ice I fuppofe had broken up
above, for it was driving in vaft Quantities.

There was no Way for getting over but on a Raft :
Which we-fet about, with but one poor Hatchet,
and finifhed juft after Sun-fetting. This was a whole
Day's Work : we next got it launched, and went on
Board of it : Then fet-off. But before wewere Half
Way over, we were jammed in the Ice, in fuch a
Manner that we expected every Moment our Raft to
fink, and ourfelves to perifh. I put-out my fetting
Pole to try to ftop the Raft, that the Ice might pafs
by ; when the Rapidity of the Stream threw it with

fo

fo much Violence againſt the Pole, that it jirked me
out into ten Feet Water: But I fortunately ſaved
myſelf by catching hold of one of the Raft Logs.
Notwithſtanding all our Efforts we could not get
the Raft to either Shore ; but were obliged, as we
were near an Iſland, to quit our Raft and make to it.

The Cold was ſo extremely ſevere, that Mr. *Giſt*
had all his Fingers, and ſome of his Toes frozen ;
and the Water was ſhut up ſo hard, that we found
no Difficulty in getting-off the Iſland, on the Ice, in
the Morning, and went to Mr. *Frazier*'s. We met
here with 20 Warriors who were going to the *South-
ward* to War : But coming to a Place upon the Head
of the great *Kunnaway*, where they found ſeven People killed and ſcalped (all but one Woman with
very light Hair) they turned about and ran back
for Fear the Inhabitants ſhould riſe and take them
as the Authors of the Murder. They report that
the Bodies were lying about the Houſe, and ſome
of them much torn and eaten by Hogs : By the
Marks which were left, they ſay they were *French*
Indians of the *Ottoway* Nation, &c. who did it.

As we intended to take Horſes here, and it required ſome Time to find them, I went-up about
three Miles to the Mouth of *Yaughyaughgane* to viſit
Queen *Alliquippa*, who had expreſſed great Concern
that we paſſed her in going to the Fort. I made
her a Preſent of a Matchcoat and a Bottle of Rum ;
which latter was thought much the beſt Preſent of
the two.

Tueſday the 1ſt Day of *January*, we left Mr.
Frazier's Houſe, and arrived at Mr. *Giſt*'s at *Monongahela* the 2d, where I bought a Horſe, Saddle,
&c. the 6th we met 17 Horſes loaded with Materi-
als and Stores for a Fort at the Forks of *Ohio*, and
the Day after ſome Families going-out to ſettle :

This

This Day we arrived at *Wills* Creek, after as fatiguing a Journey as it is poffible to conceive, rendered fo by exceffive bad Weather. From the firft Day of *December* to the 15th, there was but one Day on which it did not rain or fnow inceffantly; and throughout the whole Journey we met-with no-thing but one continued Series of cold wet Weather, which occafioned very uncomfortable Lodgings; efpecially after we had quitted our Tent, which was fome Scfeen from the Inclemency of it.

On the 11th I got to *Belvoir*; where I ftopped one Day to take neceffary Reft; and then fet out, and arrived in *Williamfburgh* the 16th; when I waited upon his Honour the Governor with the Letter I had brought from the *French* Commandant; and to give an Account of the Succefs of my Proceedings. This I beg Leave to do by offering the foregoing Narrative as it contains the moft remarkable Occurrences which happened in my Journey.

I hope what has been faid will be fufficient to make your Honour fatisfied with my Conduct; for that was my Aim in undertaking the Journey, and chief Study throughout the Profecution of it.

With the Hope of doing it, I, with infinite Pleafure fubfcribe myfelf,

Your Honour's moft Obedient,

And very humble Servant,

G. Wafhington.

C O P Y

COPY of his Honour the GOVERNOR's *Letter, to the Commandant of the* French *Forces on the* OHIO, *sent by Major* Washington.

S I R,

THE Lands upon the River *Ohio,* in the Weftern Parts of the Colony of *Virginia,* are fo notorioufly known to be the Property of the Crown of *Great-Britain* ; that it is a Matter of equal Concern and Surprize to me, to hear that a Body of *French* Forces are erecting Fortreffes, and making Settlements upon that River, within his Majefty's Dominions.

The many and repeated Complaints I have received of thefe Acts of Hoftility, lay me under the Neceffity, of fending, in the Name of the King my Mafter, the Bearer hereof, *George Washington,* Efq; one of the Adjutants General of the Forces of this Dominion; to complain to you of the Encroachments thus made, and of the Injuries done to the Subjects of *Great-Britain,* in open Violation of the Law of Nations, and the Treaties now fubfifting between the two Crowns.

If thefe Facts are true, and you fhall think fit to juftify your Proceedings, I muft defire you to acquaint me, by whofe Authority and Inftructions you have lately marched from *Canada,* with an armed Force ; and invaded the King of *Great-Britain's*

Britain's Territories, in the Manner complained of? that according to the Purport and Resolution of your Answer, I may act agreeably to the Commission I am honoured with, from the King my Master.

However Sir, in Obedience to my Instructions, it becomes my Duty to require your peaceable Departure; and that you would forbear prosecuting a Purpose so interruptive of the Harmony and good Understanding, which his Majesty is desirous to continue and cultivate with the most Christian King.

I persuade myself you will receive and entertain Major *Washington* with the Candour and Politeness natural to your Nation; and it will give me the greatest Satisfaction, if you return him with an Answer suitable to my Wishes for a very long and lasting Peace between us. I have the Honour to subscribe myself,

　　　S I R,

　　　　Your most obedient,

　　　　Humble Servant,

　　　　ROBERT DINWIDDIE.

Williamsburgh, in *Virginia*,￭
　　October 31st, 1753.

　　　　　　　T R A N S-

TRANSLATION of a Letter from Mr.
Legardeur de St. Piere, *a principal* French
Officer, in Anſwer to the Governor's Letter.

S I R,

AS I have the Honour of commanding here in
Chief, Mr. *Waſhington* delivered me the
Letter which you wrote to the Commandant of the
French Troops.

I ſhould have been glad that you had given him
Orders, or that he had been inclined to proceed to
Canada, to ſee our General ; to whom it better belongs than to me to ſet-forth the Evidence and Rea-
lity of the Rights of the King, my Maſter, upon
the Lands ſituated along the River *Ohio*, and to
conteſt the Pretenſions of the King of *Great-Britain*
thereto.

I ſhall tranſmit your Letter to the Marquis *Du-
guiſne*. His Anſwer will be a Law to me ; and if he
ſhall order me to communicate it to you, Sir, you
may be aſſured I ſhall not fail to diſpatch it to you
forthwith.

As to the Summons you ſend me to retire, I do
not think myſelf obliged to obey it. Whatever may
be your Inſtructions, I am here by Virtue of the
Orders of my General ; and I intreat you, Sir, not
to doubt one Moment, but that I am determin'd
to conform myſelf to them with all the Exactneſs
and

and Refolution which can be expected from the beft Officer.

I don't know that in the Progrefs of this Campaign any Thing has paffed which can be reputed an Act of Hoftility, or that is contrary to the Treaties which fubfift between the two Crowns; the Continuation whereof as much interefts, and is as pleafing to us, as the *Englifh*. Had you been pleafed, Sir, to have defcended to particularize the Facts which occafioned your Complaint, I fhould have had the Honour of anfwering you in the fulleft, and, I am perfuaded, moft fatisfactory Manner.

I made it my particular Care to receive Mr. *Wafhington*, with a Diftinction fuitable to your Dignity, as well as his own Quality and great Merit. I flatter myfelf that he will do me this Juftice before you, Sir ; and that he will fignify to you in the Manner I do myfelf, the profound Refpect with which I am,

S I R,

Your moft humble, and

moft obedient Servant,

LEGARDEUR DE ST. PIERE.

From the Fort fur La Riviere au Beuf, *the* 15*th of* December 1753.